OUR WEDDING DAY

1st Anniversary

____ / ____ / ____

PAPER

HOW WE CELEBRATED

_____

_____

MILESTONES THAT HAPPENED

_____

_____

_____

SHOWS WE WATCHED

_____

_____

_____

PLACES WE TRAVELED

_____

_____

_____

WHERE WE WORKED

_____

_____

4X6 PHOTO

WHERE WE LIVED

_____

_____

THE PEOPLE IN OUR FAMILY ARE

_____

_____

WHERE WE THINK WE WILL WE BE NEXT YEAR

_____

_____

_____

_____

_____

_____

2nd Anniversary

_____ / _____ / _____

COTTON

HOW WE CELEBRATED

_____

_____

MILESTONES THAT HAPPENED

_____

_____

_____

SHOWS WE WATCHED

_____

_____

_____

PLACES WE TRAVELED

_____

_____

_____

WHERE WE WORKED

_____

_____

WHERE WE LIVED

_____

_____

THE PEOPLE IN OUR FAMILY ARE

_____

_____

WHERE WE THINK WE WILL WE BE NEXT YEAR

_____

_____

_____

_____

_____

_____

3rd Anniversary

_____ / _____ / _____

LEATHER

HOW WE CELEBRATED

_____

_____

MILESTONES THAT HAPPENED

_____

_____

_____

SHOWS WE WATCHED

_____

_____

_____

PLACES WE TRAVELED

_____

_____

_____

WHERE WE WORKED

_____

_____

WHERE WE LIVED

_____

_____

THE PEOPLE IN OUR FAMILY ARE

_____

_____

WHERE WE THINK WE WILL WE BE NEXT YEAR

_____

_____

_____

_____

_____

_____

_____

4th Anniversary

____ / ____ / ____

FRUIT OR
FLOWERS

HOW WE CELEBRATED

_____

_____

MILESTONES THAT HAPPENED

_____

_____

_____

SHOWS WE WATCHED

_____

_____

_____

PLACES WE TRAVELED

_____

_____

_____

WHERE WE WORKED

_____

_____

4X6 PHOTO

WHERE WE LIVED

_____

_____

THE PEOPLE IN OUR FAMILY ARE

_____

_____

WHERE WE THINK WE WILL WE BE NEXT YEAR

_____

_____

_____

_____

_____

_____

5th Anniversary

_____ / _____ / _____

WOOD

HOW WE CELEBRATED

_____

_____

MILESTONES THAT HAPPENED

_____

_____

_____

SHOWS WE WATCHED

_____

_____

_____

PLACES WE TRAVELED

_____

_____

_____

WHERE WE WORKED

_____

_____

WHERE WE LIVED

_____

_____

THE PEOPLE IN OUR FAMILY ARE

_____

_____

WHERE WE THINK WE WILL WE BE NEXT YEAR

_____

_____

_____

_____

_____

_____

6th
Anniversary

____ / ____ / ____

HOW WE CELEBRATED

_____
_____

MILESTONES THAT HAPPENED

_____
_____
_____

SHOWS WE WATCHED

_____
_____
_____

PLACES WE TRAVELED

_____
_____
_____

WHERE WE WORKED

_____
_____

4X6 PHOTO

WHERE WE LIVED

_____

_____

THE PEOPLE IN OUR FAMILY ARE

_____

_____

WHERE WE THINK WE WILL WE BE NEXT YEAR

_____

_____

_____

_____

_____

_____

7th Anniversary

_____ / _____ / _____

WOOL OR COPPER

HOW WE CELEBRATED

_____

_____

MILESTONES THAT HAPPENED

_____

_____

_____

SHOWS WE WATCHED

_____

_____

_____

PLACES WE TRAVELED

_____

_____

_____

WHERE WE WORKED

_____

_____

4X6 PHOTO

WHERE WE LIVED

_____

_____

THE PEOPLE IN OUR FAMILY ARE

_____

_____

WHERE WE THINK WE WILL WE BE NEXT YEAR

_____

_____

_____

_____

_____

_____

8th
Anniversary

____ / ____ / ____

BRONZE

HOW WE CELEBRATED

_____

_____

MILESTONES THAT HAPPENED

_____

_____

_____

SHOWS WE WATCHED

_____

_____

_____

PLACES WE TRAVELED

_____

_____

_____

WHERE WE WORKED

_____

_____

WHERE WE LIVED

_____

_____

THE PEOPLE IN OUR FAMILY ARE

_____

_____

WHERE WE THINK WE WILL WE BE NEXT YEAR

_____

_____

_____

_____

_____

_____

9th Anniversary

_____ / _____ / _____

POTTERY

HOW WE CELEBRATED

_____

_____

MILESTONES THAT HAPPENED

_____

_____

_____

SHOWS WE WATCHED

_____

_____

_____

PLACES WE TRAVELED

_____

_____

_____

WHERE WE WORKED

_____

_____

WHERE WE LIVED

_____

_____

THE PEOPLE IN OUR FAMILY ARE

_____

_____

WHERE WE THINK WE WILL WE BE NEXT YEAR

_____

_____

_____

_____

_____

_____

10th Anniversary

___ / ___ / ___

HOW WE CELEBRATED

_____

_____

MILESTONES THAT HAPPENED

_____

_____

_____

SHOWS WE WATCHED

_____

_____

_____

PLACES WE TRAVELED

_____

_____

_____

WHERE WE WORKED

_____

_____

4X6 PHOTO

WHERE WE LIVED

_____

_____

THE PEOPLE IN OUR FAMILY ARE

_____

_____

WHERE WE THINK WE WILL WE BE NEXT YEAR

_____

_____

_____

_____

_____

_____

11th Anniversary

____ / ____ / ____

STEEL

HOW WE CELEBRATED

_____

_____

MILESTONES THAT HAPPENED

_____

_____

_____

SHOWS WE WATCHED

_____

_____

_____

PLACES WE TRAVELED

_____

_____

_____

WHERE WE WORKED

_____

_____

4X6 PHOTO

WHERE WE LIVED

_____

_____

THE PEOPLE IN OUR FAMILY ARE

_____

_____

WHERE WE THINK WE WILL WE BE NEXT YEAR

_____

_____

_____

_____

_____

_____

12th Anniversary

___ / ___ / ___

SILK OR LINEN

HOW WE CELEBRATED

_____
_____

MILESTONES THAT HAPPENED

_____
_____
_____

SHOWS WE WATCHED

_____
_____
_____

PLACES WE TRAVELED

_____
_____
_____

WHERE WE WORKED

_____
_____

4X6 PHOTO

WHERE WE LIVED

_____

_____

THE PEOPLE IN OUR FAMILY ARE

_____

_____

WHERE WE THINK WE WILL WE BE NEXT YEAR

_____

_____

_____

_____

_____

13th Anniversary

____ / ____ / ____

LACE

HOW WE CELEBRATED

_____

_____

MILESTONES THAT HAPPENED

_____

_____

_____

SHOWS WE WATCHED

_____

_____

_____

PLACES WE TRAVELED

_____

_____

_____

WHERE WE WORKED

_____

_____

4X6 PHOTO

WHERE WE LIVED

_____

_____

THE PEOPLE IN OUR FAMILY ARE

_____

_____

WHERE WE THINK WE WILL WE BE NEXT YEAR

_____

_____

_____

_____

_____

_____

14th Anniversary

_____ / _____ / _____

IVORY

HOW WE CELEBRATED

_____

_____

MILESTONES THAT HAPPENED

_____

_____

_____

SHOWS WE WATCHED

_____

_____

_____

PLACES WE TRAVELED

_____

_____

_____

WHERE WE WORKED

_____

_____

4X6 PHOTO

WHERE WE LIVED

_____

_____

THE PEOPLE IN OUR FAMILY ARE

_____

_____

WHERE WE THINK WE WILL WE BE NEXT YEAR

_____

_____

_____

_____

_____

_____

15th Anniversary

____ / ____ / ____

CRYSTAL

HOW WE CELEBRATED

_____

_____

MILESTONES THAT HAPPENED

_____

_____

_____

SHOWS WE WATCHED

_____

_____

_____

PLACES WE TRAVELED

_____

_____

_____

WHERE WE WORKED

_____

_____

WHERE WE LIVED

_____

_____

THE PEOPLE IN OUR FAMILY ARE

_____

_____

WHERE WE THINK WE WILL WE BE NEXT YEAR

_____

_____

_____

_____

_____

_____

16th Anniversary

___ / ___ / ___

WAX

HOW WE CELEBRATED

_____

_____

MILESTONES THAT HAPPENED

_____

_____

_____

SHOWS WE WATCHED

_____

_____

_____

PLACES WE TRAVELED

_____

_____

_____

WHERE WE WORKED

_____

_____

WHERE WE LIVED

_____

_____

THE PEOPLE IN OUR FAMILY ARE

_____

_____

WHERE WE THINK WE WILL WE BE NEXT YEAR

_____

_____

_____

_____

_____

_____

17th Anniversary

_____ / _____ / _____

FURNITURE

HOW WE CELEBRATED

_____

_____

MILESTONES THAT HAPPENED

_____

_____

_____

SHOWS WE WATCHED

_____

_____

_____

PLACES WE TRAVELED

_____

_____

_____

WHERE WE WORKED

_____

_____

4X6 PHOTO

WHERE WE LIVED

_____

_____

THE PEOPLE IN OUR FAMILY ARE

_____

_____

WHERE WE THINK WE WILL WE BE NEXT YEAR

_____

_____

_____

_____

_____

_____

_____

18th Anniversary

_____ / _____ / _____

PORCELAIN

HOW WE CELEBRATED

_____

_____

MILESTONES THAT HAPPENED

_____

_____

_____

SHOWS WE WATCHED

_____

_____

_____

PLACES WE TRAVELED

_____

_____

_____

WHERE WE WORKED

_____

_____

4X6 PHOTO

WHERE WE LIVED

_____

_____

THE PEOPLE IN OUR FAMILY ARE

_____

_____

WHERE WE THINK WE WILL WE BE NEXT YEAR

_____

_____

_____

_____

_____

_____

19th Anniversary

___ / ___ / ___

BRONZE

HOW WE CELEBRATED

_____

_____

MILESTONES THAT HAPPENED

_____

_____

_____

SHOWS WE WATCHED

_____

_____

_____

PLACES WE TRAVELED

_____

_____

_____

WHERE WE WORKED

_____

_____

WHERE WE LIVED

_____

_____

THE PEOPLE IN OUR FAMILY ARE

_____

_____

WHERE WE THINK WE WILL WE BE NEXT YEAR

_____

_____

_____

_____

_____

_____

20th Anniversary

_____ / _____ / _____

CHINA

HOW WE CELEBRATED

_____

_____

MILESTONES THAT HAPPENED

_____

_____

_____

SHOWS WE WATCHED

_____

_____

_____

PLACES WE TRAVELED

_____

_____

_____

WHERE WE WORKED

_____

_____

4X6 PHOTO

WHERE WE LIVED

_____

_____

THE PEOPLE IN OUR FAMILY ARE

_____

_____

WHERE WE THINK WE WILL WE BE NEXT YEAR

_____

_____

_____

_____

_____

_____

21st Anniversary

_____ / _____ / _____

HOW WE CELEBRATED

_____

_____

MILESTONES THAT HAPPENED

_____

_____

_____

SHOWS WE WATCHED

_____

_____

_____

PLACES WE TRAVELED

_____

_____

_____

WHERE WE WORKED

_____

_____

4X6 PHOTO

WHERE WE LIVED

_____

_____

THE PEOPLE IN OUR FAMILY ARE

_____

_____

WHERE WE THINK WE WILL WE BE NEXT YEAR

_____

_____

_____

_____

_____

_____

22nd Anniversary

____ / ____ / ____

HOW WE CELEBRATED

_____

_____

MILESTONES THAT HAPPENED

_____

_____

_____

SHOWS WE WATCHED

_____

_____

_____

PLACES WE TRAVELED

_____

_____

_____

WHERE WE WORKED

_____

_____

WHERE WE LIVED

_____

_____

THE PEOPLE IN OUR FAMILY ARE

_____

_____

WHERE WE THINK WE WILL WE BE NEXT YEAR

_____

_____

_____

_____

_____

_____

23rd Anniversary

____ / ____ / ____

HOW WE CELEBRATED

_____

_____

MILESTONES THAT HAPPENED

_____

_____

_____

SHOWS WE WATCHED

_____

_____

_____

PLACES WE TRAVELED

_____

_____

_____

WHERE WE WORKED

_____

_____

WHERE WE LIVED

_____

_____

THE PEOPLE IN OUR FAMILY ARE

_____

_____

WHERE WE THINK WE WILL WE BE NEXT YEAR

_____

_____

_____

_____

_____

_____

24th Anniversary

_____ / _____ / _____

HOW WE CELEBRATED

_____

_____

MILESTONES THAT HAPPENED

_____

_____

_____

SHOWS WE WATCHED

_____

_____

_____

PLACES WE TRAVELED

_____

_____

_____

WHERE WE WORKED

_____

_____

WHERE WE LIVED

_____

_____

THE PEOPLE IN OUR FAMILY ARE

_____

_____

WHERE WE THINK WE WILL WE BE NEXT YEAR

_____

_____

_____

_____

_____

_____

25th Anniversary

_____ / _____ / _____

SILVER

HOW WE CELEBRATED

_____

_____

MILESTONES THAT HAPPENED

_____

_____

_____

SHOWS WE WATCHED

_____

_____

_____

PLACES WE TRAVELED

_____

_____

_____

WHERE WE WORKED

_____

_____

WHERE WE LIVED

_____

_____

THE PEOPLE IN OUR FAMILY ARE

_____

_____

WHERE WE THINK WE WILL WE BE NEXT YEAR

_____

_____

_____

_____

_____

_____

26th Anniversary

____ / ____ / ____

HOW WE CELEBRATED

_____

_____

MILESTONES THAT HAPPENED

_____

_____

_____

SHOWS WE WATCHED

_____

_____

_____

PLACES WE TRAVELED

_____

_____

_____

WHERE WE WORKED

_____

_____

4X6 PHOTO

WHERE WE LIVED

_____

_____

THE PEOPLE IN OUR FAMILY ARE

_____

_____

WHERE WE THINK WE WILL WE BE NEXT YEAR

_____

_____

_____

_____

_____

_____

27th Anniversary

____ / ____ / ____

HOW WE CELEBRATED

_____

_____

MILESTONES THAT HAPPENED

_____

_____

_____

SHOWS WE WATCHED

_____

_____

_____

PLACES WE TRAVELED

_____

_____

_____

WHERE WE WORKED

_____

_____

4X6 PHOTO

WHERE WE LIVED

_____

_____

THE PEOPLE IN OUR FAMILY ARE

_____

_____

WHERE WE THINK WE WILL WE BE NEXT YEAR

_____

_____

_____

_____

_____

_____

28th Anniversary

___ / ___ / ___

HOW WE CELEBRATED

_____

_____

MILESTONES THAT HAPPENED

_____

_____

_____

SHOWS WE WATCHED

_____

_____

_____

PLACES WE TRAVELED

_____

_____

_____

WHERE WE WORKED

_____

_____

WHERE WE LIVED

_____

_____

THE PEOPLE IN OUR FAMILY ARE

_____

_____

WHERE WE THINK WE WILL WE BE NEXT YEAR

_____

_____

_____

_____

_____

_____

29th Anniversary

_____ / _____ / _____

HOW WE CELEBRATED

_____

_____

MILESTONES THAT HAPPENED

_____

_____

_____

SHOWS WE WATCHED

_____

_____

_____

PLACES WE TRAVELED

_____

_____

_____

WHERE WE WORKED

_____

_____

4X6 PHOTO

WHERE WE LIVED

_____

_____

THE PEOPLE IN OUR FAMILY ARE

_____

_____

WHERE WE THINK WE WILL WE BE NEXT YEAR

_____

_____

_____

_____

_____

_____

30th Anniversary

___ / ___ / ___

PEARLS

HOW WE CELEBRATED

_____

_____

MILESTONES THAT HAPPENED

_____

_____

_____

SHOWS WE WATCHED

_____

_____

_____

PLACES WE TRAVELED

_____

_____

_____

WHERE WE WORKED

_____

_____

WHERE WE LIVED

_____

_____

THE PEOPLE IN OUR FAMILY ARE

_____

_____

WHERE WE THINK WE WILL WE BE NEXT YEAR

_____

_____

_____

_____

_____

_____

Made in the USA
Middletown, DE
15 October 2023

40850556R00035